Managing Change

Pocket Mentor Series

The *Pocket Mentor* Series offers immediate solutions to common challenges managers face on the job every day. Each book in the series is packed with handy tools, self-tests, and real-life examples to help you identify your strengths and weaknesses and hone critical skills. Whether you're at your desk, in a meeting, or on the road, these portable guides enable you to tackle the daily demands of your work with greater speed, savvy, and effectiveness.

Books in the series:

Managing
Change
Expert Solutions to
Everyday Challenges

Harvard Business Press

Boston, Massachusetts

Copyright 2009 Harvard Business School Publishing
All rights reserved
Printed in the United States of America
11 10 9 8 7 6 5 4 3

Library of Congress Cataloging-in-Publication Data

Managing change.
       p. cm. — (Pocket mentor series)
   Includes bibliographical references.
   ISBN 978-1-4221-2969-2 (pbk.)
  1. Organizational change—Management.
   HD58.8.M25434 2009
   658.4'06—dc22

                              2009019395

Contents

Implementing a Change Program   29

Powerful tactics for executing change.

Communicating About Change   37

How to discuss change effectively with your employees.

Managing Reactions to Change   45

Tips for understanding and handling employees' responses to a change initiative.

Maintaining Your Effectiveness During Change   55

Suggestions for safeguarding your own health and productivity.

Tips and Tools

Tools for Managing Change   63

Worksheets to help you assess your effectiveness as a change leader, communicate about change with your team, address any resistance to change from your group, and overcome common obstacles to change.

Test Yourself   71

A helpful review of concepts presented in this guide. Take it before and after you've read the guide, to see how much you've learned.

To Learn More   77

Further titles of articles and books if you want to go more deeply into the topic.

Sources for Managing Change   83

Notes   85

For you to use as ideas come to mind.

Mentor's Message: Why Managing Change Effectively Is Important

In today's ever more competitive and challenging business environment, organizations need to change on a fairly constant basis to survive and to fulfill their mission. That's true for all types of organizations—corporations, not-for-profit entities, and government agencies.

But change—whether it takes the form of a major restructuring, adoption of a new business process, or a modification of how a company measures performance—isn't easy. It can be scary for employees at all levels in the organization. It's almost always disruptive. And it's difficult to implement. (It's one thing to say, "We need to win back customers by improving our service to them." It's quite another to actually *make* those improvements.)

Still, managing change effectively *is* possible. This book will help you with a wealth of ideas, tools, and examples you can use to master the most challenging aspects of leading a change initiative—from helping your team become change-ready and implementing a change effort to communicating about change, managing resistance, and maintaining an even keel yourself during a difficult change process.

Learn how to lead change effectively, and you'll help position your group—and your entire organization—to adapt to whatever forces are reshaping your particular industry or sector.

Linda A. Hill, Mentor

During more than twenty years of extensive field work, Professor Linda A. Hill has helped managers create the conditions for effective management in today's flatter and increasingly diverse organizations. She is a professor and chair of the Leadership Initiative at Harvard Business School. She is also the author of the best-selling *Becoming a Manager* (Harvard Business Press), now in paperback. Hill served as the content expert for *Coaching for Results* and *Managing Direct Reports,* two award-winning interactive programs from Harvard Business School Publishing. She also serves as a mentor for many Harvard ManageMentor topics.

Managing Change: The Basics

A Closer Look
at Change

There's a lot of talk about change in the workplace and in the business press. But what is change in the context of business? What forms does it take? What triggers it? And what are the defining characteristics of managers who lead change effectively in their teams? In the following pages, we explore these questions.

Types of change

In order to respond to the challenges of new competitors, markets, and technologies, organizations must undergo continual change. Some change programs are strategic in nature; for example, "Our company will now seek to expand into new markets." Others are more operational; for instance, "We need to install a better enterprise resource planning system in our organization." Some are radical and take place only once. Examples of this type of change might include a major acquisition. Other changes are more incremental, purposefully paced to promote continuous improvement and stability. Examples might include gradual implementation of a new performance-management methodology over many years.

Change programs can take various forms. For example, a program may be designed to reconfigure an organization—through a merger, acquisition, consolidation, or divestiture—to achieve greater overall performance. It may focus on elimination of nonessential activities to reduce operational costs. It may concentrate on altering how business processes are carried out in the organization to achieve new efficiencies. A change initiative may be intended to alter a company's operating values or norms of behavior, in other words, its culture. Or it may seek to define a new strategic direction, for instance, expanding from local to global markets.

Clearly, change can take many different forms. It also can be prompted by a variety of different forces.

Sources of change

While external forces, such as an economic downturn or the introduction of new legislative laws, can cause a company to change, most changes that occur within an organization are generated from within. Managers at all levels in an organization can and do initiate change. Frontline managers, for example, may implement a new technology that requires people to carry out their job activities differently. Mid-level managers may create a plan to reduce costs. And senior managers may decide to merge the company with another organization.

What lies behind us and what lies before us are tiny matters compared with what lies within us.
    —Oliver Wendell Holmes

Characteristics of effective change leaders

Regardless of the type of change and the source, change is almost always disruptive and, at times, traumatic. Because of this, many people try to avoid it. Nevertheless, change is part of organizational life and essential for progress. Accepting the necessity and inevitability of change enables managers to see times of transition not as threats, but as opportunities for reinventing their companies and themselves. Managers who approach change with open minds and focus on its positive elements find ways to motivate others and harness enthusiasm for further progress.

Whether managers are asked to carry out a change program initiated by senior management or whether they initiate a change program within their own unit or group, successful change leaders share these common characteristics:

- They are seen by others as trustworthy and competent.

- They have a big-picture perspective; they understand the long-range strategy for their organization and unit.

- They have a clear, compelling vision of the change they want to see happen.

- They can articulate what the change is, why it is necessary, and how it will benefit employees and the organization overall.

- They are able to identify the people who can make the change a reality, and they know how to get their support and cooperation.

- They are able to align and engage team members who'll need to embrace the change and stakeholders whose support is also necessary.

- They can motivate others to achieve the change vision.

- They see opportunities in change and can diagnose problems with a change initiative from their direct reports' and other stakeholders' perspectives.

- They are able to eliminate barriers that interfere with the change initiative.

Although it is impossible to anticipate every change effort, the likelihood of change is something managers can count on—and plan for. Managers who know how to anticipate, catalyze, and effect change will find their careers, and their experience in their companies, more satisfying and successful.

One key to leading change effectively is to help your team become change-ready—perpetually prepared to adopt changes needed to meet strategic goals and keep the organization competitive.

Helping Your Team Become Change-Ready

mployees and teams who are change-ready are able to leap into action when needed to effect required change. To help your group become ready for change, you first need to understand the defining characteristics of change-readiness and then apply specific practices to build preparedness into your team's culture.

Understanding the characteristics of change-readiness

For any organization (whether an entire company, a division, a department, or a team) to successfully implement change, it must be change-ready—meaning that the organization's people, structures, and processes are prepared for and capable of change. How do you know when *your* organization is change-ready? Typically, three conditions are present.

First, **effective leadership is in place at all levels in the organization**. Inept leaders are deterrents to organizational performance and constrain the organization's ability to change. A company may have excellent pay, benefits, and employee-friendly policies, but if incompetent leaders are in place, its employees will not be motivated to change.

Second, **employees are personally motivated to change**. Change happens when people are sufficiently dissatisfied with the status quo and are willing to make the effort and to accept the risks involved in doing something new or carrying out work processes differently.

Third, **the organization is accustomed to working collaboratively**. Effective change demands collaboration between willing and motivated parties. People from different parts and different levels of the organization cooperate to set goals, alter the way things are done, and push the organization toward the new and better future state promised by the change program.

Preparing your employees for change

Change-readiness doesn't happen automatically. A manager must cultivate it. If you manage a division, business unit, department, or group, there are certain steps you can take to help your organization become change-ready. The following suggestions can help:

Take stock of your group's current culture. Start by understanding the culture you inherited when you first began managing your group or department. What are people's attitudes toward change? For example, are they generally happy with the way things are now? What would they like to see change? What would they like to see remain the same? How will the change program you'll be leading affect them—their jobs, their relationships, their feelings about the company?

By assessing these aspects of your group's current culture, you can gain a sense of how change-ready your people may be. If they're already very open to change, you may find it relatively easy to introduce alterations to how your people do their work. If

What Would YOU Do?

Resistance Brewing at New Brew

OR TEN YEARS, New Brew Coffee was a privately run company. The long-standing culture was laid-back and informal, with few hierarchical reporting structures. Last year, New Brew went public, and everything changed. The company hired new people, creating additional layers of management and several new divisions. It initiated new policies and procedures, such as stricter work-scheduling rules. And it established new goals, including specific increases in revenue. Veteran employees—those who had been with New Brew since the beginning—were having a tough time dealing with all the changes.

When Debra, the new head of the freshly created ancillary-products division, asked all managers in her department to submit detailed weekly status reports on the projects their teams were responsible for, she encountered significant resistance. One manager said, "I don't have time to do these reports. We've got work to do here!" Debra couldn't understand why her managers were responding this way: didn't they see that being a publicly owned company required more efficient and transparent record keeping? How could she hope to establish an effective record-keeping system in a culture that resisted formal structures?

they're not at all change-ready, you'll need to make a bigger effort to help them become so.

Assess your own credibility. Your people will find it easier to embrace a change you're proposing if they view you as credible. That is, they believe that you've made smart choices about the change program and that you have the organization's and the group's best interests at heart. They respect your judgment and wisdom.

If you lack credibility before launching a change initiative, you can strengthen it through several means. For example, build relationships with key individuals in your group—star performers and employees who are most amenable to change and who will be willing to back you when you launch your change program. You might also consider building a coalition around your change initiative—a coterie of people who are excited about the proposed change and can stir up enthusiasm for it among their colleagues.

Encourage participative work within your unit. Develop more participative approaches to how everyday business is handled. Specifically:

- Push decision making down to lowest levels possible. Allowing others to make informed decisions, rather than imposing your own decisions on others, increases group members' perception of their own effectiveness—and yours.

- Share information freely. Information is the lifeblood of any organization. During times of change, getting and disseminating information are critical to operating effectively, flexibly, and quickly.

- Make communication a two way process. Talk but also listen, especially to people who are resistant to change.

- Get into the trenches with frontline employees to better understand the day-to-day issues that they face.

- Give people practice in collaborative work between functions by tackling problems and assigning projects through cross-functional teams.

- Help people see the "why" of change.

Give your employees a voice. Employees who can freely express their ideas will feel more empowered to act. To that end, encourage people to openly discuss their thoughts and feelings about the change program you're advocating. Work to understand resistance by exploring their concerns and by taking their feelings seriously. When people believe that their voice counts, they are more apt to mobilize for change.

Drive fear out of your group. An organizational culture dominated by fear is incapable of serious change. Fear encourages everyone to avoid risks, to become internally focused, and to stop

What You COULD Do

> Remember Debra's concern about how to introduce a new record-keeping process in her division at New Brew?

Here's what the mentor suggests:

To get everyone on the right track, Debra might have spoken with each of the department managers to better understand how they currently keep records within their groups and how they share information with others in the company. She might then have explained the need for greater accountability and asked them for suggestions on how to improve existing practices. Next, Debra might have framed the new plan as an experiment, one that would be modified over time in response to feedback. By asking for input and agreeing to modify the trial plan, Debra would have boosted the odds of enlisting her people's help in improving record keeping and reaching her desired outcome.

communicating—all of which constrains the ability to change. In addition, fear costs organizations real money in the form of increased absenteeism, reduced productivity, and diminished quality of products and services.

While you should aim to reduce fear in your group, you should not deny or sugarcoat the challenging aspects of the change itself, and you should not minimize the intensity of employees' reactions to it. Instead, openly acknowledge employees' concerns and work with them to support and embrace the change initiative.

Once your organization is primed for transition through these change-readiness actions, a change initiative can be rolled out.

Six Steps to Managing Change

Y ou've taken action to cultivate change-readiness in your group. And you've identified a specific change initiative you need to implement. How do you ensure the success of your change initiative? There's no specific formula. Many managers wish there were a formula, but launching a change program is not that easy. Barriers to change abound; poor leadership, lack of collaboration and teamwork, paralyzing company politics, and fear of the unknown are just a few examples.

Yet envisioning change as a specific set of steps can help you take a disciplined approach and overcome the many barriers to a successful rollout. Here's a preview of a six-step model many companies have found useful:

1. Mobilize energy and commitment by identifying business problems and solutions.

2. Develop and communicate a shared vision of the change program.

3. Identify the change program's leadership.

4. Create short-term wins by focusing on results, not activities.

5. Institutionalize success through formal processes, systems, and structures.

6. Monitor and adjust strategies in response to problems in the change process.

We'll explore these steps in greater detail next. Then, we'll examine a set of practices that, if used during this six-step process, can further strengthen your effectiveness at leading change in your group.

Step 1: Mobilize your team's energy

You mobilize your team's energy and commitment by identifying business problems and solutions. Indeed, the starting point of *any* effective change effort is a clear definition of the business problem that the proposed change intends to address. Problem identification answers the most important question employees will ask: why must we undergo change? Your answer lays the foundation for motivating all employees in your organization and thus must be convincing.

Here are some examples of business problems requiring change:

- "A new competitor has begun to take market share away from us. We won't stay in business too much longer if this continues."

- "Customers are demanding increased speed and greater reliability in our service to them. Many of them have defected to rival companies that provide higher-quality service."

- "To gain the new capabilities as well as cost and revenue synergies we need to remain competitive in this tough business climate, we're going to acquire two companies. That's going to mean some major structural, procedural, and cultural changes to make the postmerger integration pay off as planned."

Informing people why change must occur is essential not only for its motivating potential, but also for creating a much-needed sense of urgency. Simply put, change won't happen without a feeling of urgency. People will not grapple with the pain and extra work associated with a serious change effort unless they are convinced that maintaining the status quo is more dangerous than striking out on a new path.

After defining the business problem, the next step to mobilizing your team's energy is to develop a solution to the problem you've identified. A set of alternatives should be generated and then evaluated against the objectives of the change initiative. For instance:

- "To regain market share, we could step up our efforts to develop more innovative products as well as make our business processes more efficient."

- "To improve customer loyalty, we might explore new ways to understand how our customers use our products and our postsales services and to identify service problems more quickly."

- "To get the most value from our upcoming acquisitions, we should consider blending redundant support units and restructuring reporting relationships in the newly acquired divisions."

While identifying the business problem and its possible solutions is a must, *how* you identify them is equally important. You'll foster the greatest motivation and commitment from employees if you involve them—especially those who will be most affected by the change effort—in identifying the problem and planning its solution. Neglect this part of change leadership, and you may well end up inaccurately identifying the business problem at hand or coming up with a solution that's too narrow. You'll get the best possible range of ideas for the problem *and* its potential solution if you elicit thoughts and insights from your people as well as from yourself.

Step 2: Develop a shared vision

It isn't enough to just identify the problem and agree on how to proceed to solve it through a particular change effort. You have to get people excited about forging ahead. That means developing a clear vision of where your organization or unit needs to go, and communicating that vision to your people in ways that make the benefits of the change effort clear.

In communicating the vision, be very specific about how the change will improve the business (for example, by delivering greater customer satisfaction, product quality, or sales revenues). If possible, explain how these improvements will also benefit employees (for instance, by making it possible for people to earn higher pay, get larger bonuses, or have new opportunities for advancement).

Here are additional suggestions for developing an effective shared vision:

- Describe a desirable future, one that people would be happy to have right now if they could.

- Make the vision compelling. It must be better than the status quo, so people will gladly undertake the effort and make the sacrifices necessary to attain the vision.

- **Ensure that the vision is realistic.** People need to see the vision as being within their grasp if they work hard to make it real.

- **Focus on a manageable and coherent set of goals.** Break the vision down into objectives that people can understand and handle.

- **Build in flexibility** so that if the circumstances driving the proposed change effort shift, the vision can be modified as needed.

- **Make sure the vision is easy to communicate** to all levels of people, both inside and outside your organization.

Once you've developed a shared vision, communicate it to your employees through every means possible—including meetings, e-mails, company newsletter and Web-site articles, even everyday props (such as posters or T-shirts). Consistent, frequent communication of the vision helps ensure that all employees understand the change effort that is currently under way and the desired future it will aim to create. (See the section "Communicating about Change" for additional information on this aspect of change leadership.)

Tip: Don't underestimate the power of a vision. Without a compelling vision, a change effort can easily dissolve into a list of confusing, incompatible, and time-consuming projects that go in the wrong direction, go nowhere at all, or work at cross-purposes.

Step 3: Identify change leaders

In order for change to succeed, strong leadership must be in place at all levels in an organization, not just at the top. Leaders of change champion the change effort by assembling the resources needed for the project, and they take responsibility for its success or failure.

Often, when change programs are being rolled out, some units present themselves as more change-ready than others—that is, they have respected and effective leaders in place, employees are motivated to change, and people in those units are accustomed to working together in collaborative ways. For senior executives heading up major change programs, it's wise to roll out such a program first in these units, which can then be used as test beds for the change initiative.

If you manage a department or group, you (of course) will be the central change leader. But you can identify additional change leaders among your employees, those individuals who can step up and manage various components of the change program and thereby keep the initiative alive in your group.

Step 4: Create short-term wins

During a change initiative, many managers make the mistake of focusing their attention on training people in required new skills, forming teams and task forces to manage components of the project, and carrying out other programmatic activities that seem as though they should produce desirable results. But often, these efforts aren't linked to bottom-line performance. Thus, people have difficulty seeing their value and dedicating themselves to the effort.

To avoid this mistake, don't focus only on programmatic activities. Devote most of your attention to programs that generate measurable business results in the short term, even if your change campaign (like most) will be carried out over a much longer time.

For example, if the purpose of your change initiative is to reduce costs by 30 percent over the next three years, you might create the following goal: "Within the next six months, we will reduce fuel costs by 10 percent."

Such short-term successes help move change programs forward in the following ways:

- **They provide evidence that the sacrifices required by the change program are worthwhile.** Wins greatly help justify the near-term costs involved.

- **They reward the people involved in the change effort.** After a lot of hard work, positive feedback builds morale and motivation.

- **They help fine-tune the vision and the strategies needed to make the vision real.** Near-term wins give change leaders concrete data on the viability of their ideas.

- **They undermine cynics and self-serving resisters.** Clear improvements in performance make it difficult for people to block needed change.

- **They build momentum.** Momentum turns neutrals into supporters and reluctant supporters into active helpers.

Step 5: Institutionalize successes

Once a change program objective has been achieved, it is important to cement hard-earned gains through processes, information systems, or new reporting structures that describe how work should be done going forward.

For example, an innovative unit of an office furniture manufacturer was given the opportunity to develop a new, faster, and low-cost approach to manufacturing and fulfillment. Employees in the unit completely redesigned the furniture-building process—from order taking to delivery—basing it on digital connectivity, mass customization, and a new relationship with supply-chain partners. By the time the makeover was complete, the unit had cut the order-to-shipment cycle from eight weeks to less than one week. On-time shipments reached 99.6 percent—a remarkable achievement. Once this unit reached its goal, it institutionalized its gains through a performance measurement system that kept everyone's focus on that metric.

"How to make short-term wins effective" provides additional recommendations for getting the most from your team's near-term successes.

How to make short-term wins effective

- **Make the wins visible** so that people see firsthand that their hard work is making a difference toward change.

- **Make the wins unambiguous.** Small gains, such as conducting a productive meeting or resolving a scheduling discrepancy, are not examples of short-term wins.

- **Ensure that the wins have in fact been won** and that you're not declaring victory prematurely.

- **Make sure the wins are related to the change effort.** You'll help keep all your employees focused on the higher-level goal.

Step 6: Monitor and adjust strategies

Change programs almost never go according to plan. So, you'll need to refine your strategies in response to problems in the change process. All types of unanticipated problems within your organization can crop up as a change initiative moves forward.

For instance, suppose you've installed a new customer database in your department to support a new way of analyzing customer data. You've lined up Ben, from the human resources department, to facilitate the training sessions necessary to teach people how to use the new database. But Ben unexpectedly must take a two-month leave from the company. There's no one else immediately available to fill in for him, so the training is delayed. That means a delay in getting the new database fully operational.

Developments in the external environment can also affect what's going on inside the company, making it difficult to move a change initiative forward. For example, perhaps your company has decided to expand into a new market and has launched a change effort focused on developing new products for that market. Suddenly a new competitor appears on the horizon and is going after the same market your firm has set its sights on. Your company decides it must step up the pace in developing products for the target market.

The lesson? In leading any change effort, you need to be flexible and adaptive—able and willing to accommodate alterations in schedules, sequencing of tasks, and changes in personnel.

Implementing a
Change Program

We've examined a six-step process that many change leaders use to manage change initiatives. Next we'll consider five additional practices that, when added to the process we've just explored, can further help you execute your change initiative effectively, so it delivers the results you intended. These powerful practices are:

- Craft an implementation plan.

- Enlist key people.

- Send consistent messages.

- Develop enabling structures.

- Celebrate achievement of milestones.

Craft an implementation plan

While a vision may guide and inspire employees during a change process, an organization or unit needs an implementation plan for what to do and when and how to do it in order to put a change initiative into action. Such a plan ensures that everyone's efforts are aligned with the goals of the change program.

What are the characteristics of an effective implementation plan at the unit level? A good plan:

- **Is simple.** An overly complex plan may confuse and frustrate participants in the change effort. Make your plan clear, concise, and coherent. For example, ensure that it stipulates who is supposed to do what, and when, to carry out the change project.

- **Reflects input from people who will be affected by the intended change.** An implementation plan should not be imposed on the people asked to move it forward. Rather, the people affected should be involved in developing the plan. If people have played a part in the creation of the plan, they will be more likely to support it.

- **Is structured in achievable chunks.** Overly ambitious plans are usually doomed to failure. Build a plan that can be tackled in manageable, achievable chunks. For example, if you're initiating a new way of handling customer phone calls, break the project down into parts such as developing new scripts, training people in the new process, and determining new metrics for assessing performance in the new process.

- **Specifies roles and responsibilities.** Establishing accountability in any implementation plan is essential. Define clear roles and responsibilities from the beginning to avoid any confusion later.

- **Is flexible.** As we've seen, change programs seldom follow their planned trajectories or timetables. Thus, a good implementation plan is open to revision.

Tip: Don't impose solutions that have been suggested or developed by someone else. Instead, develop solutions with the people in the unit(s) who will be most affected by the change.

Enlist key people

As you execute your organization or unit's implementation plan, be sure to enlist the support and involvement of key employees within—and outside of—your group. This means assembling a team with the right blend of leadership skills, authority, resources, and expertise. Ask yourself the following questions to ensure the effectiveness of your team:

- Do key leaders support the change effort?

- Do members of the team have the relevant expertise to do the job and make intelligent decisions?

- Do team members have a range of differing points of view so that they can analyze and address problems creatively?

- Does the team include people with sufficient credibility to ensure that employees and management will treat decisions seriously?

- Does the team include people with demonstrated leadership skills?

- Are the team members capable of forgoing their personal immediate interests in favor of the larger organizational goal?

If you answer no to any of these questions, it might be a good idea to revisit your team choices.

Never doubt that a small group of thoughtful, committed citizens can change the world. Indeed, it is the only thing that ever has.
    —Margaret Mead

Send consistent messages

Once you have articulated the need for change convincingly and enlisted broad support, you must maintain that support through consistent behavior and messages related to the change.

For example, consider an organization that was being restructured. All divisions were asked to reduce expenses. Senior managers and unit heads set the tone by flying coach on commercial flights. Instead of hiring limousines to pick them up at the airport, they took cabs. And instead of eating overpriced meals at fancy restaurants, they dined in more modest eateries. Other managers followed suit. People within the organization quickly took notice.

You'll learn more about sending consistent messages in the next section, "Communicating About Change."

Develop enabling structures

Enabling structures are the activities and programs that underpin successful implementation and are a critical part of the overall plan; they include:

- **Pilot programs** to give people opportunities to grapple with implementation and its problems on a smaller, more manageable scale. Pilots are test beds in which implementers can experiment with change initiatives before rolling them out more broadly. For example, in one pilot program, a manager tested a new process for handling customer phone calls in a small experimental team within her unit.

- **Training programs** to provide employees with opportunities to improve their skills so that they can contribute more effectively to the change initiative.

- **Reward systems** to recognize employees who demonstrate the results and behaviors essential in order for the desired change to deliver its promised benefits. Be sure to visibly reward people who have contributed to the successful generation of short-term wins.

Enabling structures foster a sense of agency (the power to take action) and ownership that people need to feel in order to embrace change. "How to foster a sense of agency and ownership" offers additional ideas.

How to foster a sense of agency and ownership

- Demonstrate trust and respect for employees—and do it regularly.

- Encourage innovative thinking.

- Delegate and don't micromanage.

- Be flexible and demonstrate that flexibility to others.

- Encourage risk taking and be tolerant of failures.

- Spread decision-making authority around.

Celebrate achievement of milestones

Change initiatives can be frustrating and take a long time. To maintain enthusiasm for and commitment to a change program, you'll therefore need to celebrate milestones as your employees reach them. Taking the time to recognize achievements is important because it acknowledges people's hard work, boosts morale, keeps up the momentum, and neutralizes skepticism about the change effort.

Don't make the mistake of celebrating milestones *before* your employees have actually achieved them. Declaring victory prematurely will only dissipate the sense of urgency needed to keep people motivated about the change initiative.

Tip: Don't attempt to change everything at once. Often, managers try to do too much too fast. Unless the organization is in a major crisis, roll out change initiatives on a smaller scale, for example, in a team that already has strong leadership and a collaborative spirit. Once the change program takes hold, launch similar initiatives in other teams, letting change spread slowly throughout your unit or organization.

Communicating
About Change

The previous section discussed the importance of sending consistent messages while leading a change program. Next we examine communication more closely, in particular, the strategies for developing a communication plan, deciding what to communicate, and delivering the message.

Developing a communication plan

Effective communication sets the tone for the change program and is critical to implementation. Everyone—from senior management to unit and group heads—should have communication plans in place in order to help employees understand why the change is taking place, what the change program is intended to do, and how long it will take. Such plans must also specify how you'll inform employees about key decisions that have been made and changes that have been incorporated into the implementation plan.

There is no such thing as overcommunicating information about a change effort. Examine your communication plan and ask whether it stipulates how you'll keep all stakeholders informed as the change initiative moves forward. Stakeholders may include supervisors, peers, colleagues in other parts of your organization, and direct reports—as well as suppliers or vendors, shareholders, and even customers.

Deciding what to communicate

Communicating about the change program you're managing begins by looking at it from the perspective of each of your key stakeholders. Try to identify what would energize and inspire them to work toward the goals of the change effort. Specifically, they will want—and need—to know:

- **What the change program is and what it plans to do.** Define what the change is, what the organization hopes to achieve with it, how it will improve the business, and how the improvements will benefit employees.

- **Why the change is taking place.** Inform people about the business reasons underpinning the change program. Many people will not have been involved in identifying the business problems and developing solution alternatives. Share this information with your group and discuss the various options that were available and why you selected the solution you did.

- **What the scope of the change program is.** Describe how long the change program will take and discuss the implementation plan. Some people will be more affected by a particular change project than others, and the disparity might lead to fear-generating speculation. Fear and uncertainty tend to paralyze a group and stall its efforts. You can short-circuit these negative emotions by providing the facts. Be up-front and honest about the change program, even if it contains bad news. Also remind people that certain things *won't* change

What Would YOU Do?

Managing the Urge to Merge at GenCo

ARCUS IS THE HEAD of GenCo Inc.'s corporate training group. As part of a companywide change program to reduce costs, senior management has decided to merge his group with the organizational development group. He will be responsible for restructuring and managing the new department.

The two groups have markedly different emphases. Corporate training offers companywide workshops designed to help employees master specific skills, such as learning a new computer application. Organizational development focuses exclusively on high-level executive development. Corporate training uses off-the-shelf training tools, while organizational development uses outside consulting services.

The restructuring will require some people to learn new skills and others to assume new roles and responsibilities—two things that have triggered intense anxiety among employees. Marcus ponders what to say to both groups after he announces the change. Should he reassure them that there's nothing to be afraid of and that the change will be completely manageable? Emphasize the changes in roles and responsibilities that will be coming? Explain the reasons behind the change initiative?

What would YOU do? The mentor will suggest a solution in *What You COULD Do.*

and explain exactly what will remain constant throughout the effort. This will help anchor uneasy employees.

- **What hurdles stand in the way of implementation.** There are bound to be barriers to successful implementation, such as a shortage of funds, resistance from unexpected quarters, and unexpected occurrences that create delays. Help people become aware of these barriers so they can better anticipate them.

- **What the criteria for success are and how success will be measured.** Define successful implementation of the change program clearly and establish measures for what you want to accomplish. For instance, "We'll know we've made the change when we've improved on-time delivery from 80 percent to 95 percent by end of the year."

- **How people will be rewarded for success.** People need incentives for the added work and disruptions that change requires. Be very clear about how individuals will be rewarded for progress toward change goals, whether it's through monetary rewards (such as bonuses or pay increases) or nonmonetary rewards (for example, opportunities to lead a high-visibility task force, or a gift certificate to a local restaurant).

Delivering the message

When crafting your communication plan, be sure to use diverse communication channels. In addition to staff meetings, stand-up presentations, and e-mails, consider channels such as a monthly newsletter, hosted events, one-on-one meetings, and an intranet site devoted to issues surrounding the change effort. And, of course, exhibit the behaviors and attitudes you're asking others to demonstrate to support the change effort. The goal is to generate as much communication as possible to get the message of the change program across.

Above all, make communication an ongoing, two-way proposition. While it is important to share information, it is equally important to listen to what others have to say. Take the time to ask employees how they are doing and how they perceive the change program initiatives. Listening to their concerns and different points of view will help you keep everyone motivated and invested in the change program.

Tip: Don't undercommunicate the purpose of the change and actions planned. Without credible information, and a lot of it, employees won't be motivated to change.

What You COULD Do

Remember Marcus's questions about how
to communicate about the group merger
with affected employees?

Here's what the mentor suggests:

To capitalize on change, managers should share as much information as possible with employees. Sharing information means explaining the big picture behind the change initiative, such as the organization's long-range strategy. Managers should also describe the change program in terms of its benefits, both for the company and its employees. Finally, managers should acknowledge employees' anxieties. For example, allow people to express their concerns in productive ways during meetings. When employees can see the big picture, perceive the benefits offered by the change, and express their anxieties, they will be more likely to embrace and support the initiative.

Marcus might say something like the following to the employees who will be affected by the group merger: "Because of the tight economy and decreased customer spending, our entire organization needs to reduce costs. Even though the restructuring of our two groups might seem scary, it will give us important new opportunities to decrease our costs and help our company remain competitive."

Managing Reactions to Change

I n launching any change effort, you're bound to get a variety of responses from employees—everything from passionate support to determined resistance. Next we explore ways to anticipate this range of potential responses and strategies for addressing resistance to your change program.

Anticipating positive and negative responses

Even when you've taken all the steps necessary to implement a positive and successful change program, you may find that people's reactions to change vary. Organizations are social entities made up of people who have different personalities, perspectives, emotions, and levels of authority. Some people welcome the opportunities that change brings, while others fear change and don't want to let go of the status quo. As a manager, it's your job to anticipate, understand, and deal with people's individual reactions to change.

"Reactions to change" shows some of the reasons people embrace or resist change.

Addressing resistance

Resisters are commonly seen as people who refuse to accept or adapt to change. They're perceived as inflexible, unaccommodating, and lacking team spirit. As such, resisters are considered

Reactions to change

Why people support change	Why people resist change
• They believe that the change makes sense and is the right course of action.	• They believe change is unnecessary or will make the situation worse.
• They respect the people leading the change effort.	• They don't trust the people mandating or leading the change effort.
• They expect new opportunities and challenges to come from the change.	• They don't like the way the change has been introduced.
• They were involved in planning and implementing the change program.	• They are not confident the change will succeed.
• They believe that the change will result in personal gain.	• They have had no input in planning and implementing the change program.
• They enjoy the excitement of change.	• They feel that change will mean personal loss—of security, money, status, or friends.
	• They believe in the status quo.
	• They've already experienced a lot of change and can't handle any more disruption.
	• They fear they don't have the skills or competencies to do their work in new ways required by the change.

What Would YOU Do?

Resistance Is Futile—or Is It?

PENELOPE HAS SHARED information with her team about why her company is installing a new enterprise resource planning system. She has discussed the benefits of the change for both the company and its employees, and she has listened carefully to people's concerns about what the new system will mean for how they carry out their work.

She knows that the next step is to come up with creative ways to implement the change effort in her group. She asks experienced employees from her team to work with her to create a formal implementation plan. After a few weeks, the team develops a plan that defines how the new technology will affect everyone's job, specifies who will need training on the new system, and identifies new roles and responsibilities regarding use of the system.

One afternoon, Penelope overhears Charlie, an employee, talking with another employee in the hallway. It sounds as if Charlie thinks the change effort is not being well led. He ends the conversation by saying, "Things were just fine with the system we had before." Penelope returns to her office and thinks about how to handle this situation. Should she recognize that some people find change more difficult than others and give Charlie time to adjust? Ask someone in the human resources department to talk with

Charlie about how to cope more effectively with change? Tell Charlie that she overheard his comments and ask to meet with him to discuss his concerns in more detail?

What would YOU do? The mentor will suggest a solution in *What You COULD Do.*

---

obstacles to be overcome. While some resisters can undermine a change effort, it is shortsighted to think all resisters will, or even fundamentally desire to, do so.

Resistance implies energy—energy that you can work with and possibly redirect in a positive direction. Instead of viewing resistance as an obstacle, try to understand its sources and motives. Doing so may uncover opportunities for improving the change effort. Resisters may have valid concerns that need to be addressed. Put their perspectives to use for the change effort and make them a part of the solution.

If you encounter resisters, try to gain their support through the following means:

- **Encourage them to openly express their thoughts and feelings about the change program.** Then listen carefully to their concerns, exploring their fears and taking their comments seriously. Remember that there are many legitimate reasons that people resist change. Don't dismiss resistors as "bad people." Understand that there are real costs associated with change, and try to get employees to articulate what those costs might be for them.

- **Reassure them that you'll help.** For example, if an employee is resisting change because she fears she lacks the competencies to carry out her work in new ways, explain that you'll provide adequate training and other resources to ensure that she develops the needed competencies.

- **Engage them in the problem definition, planning, and implementation processes.** The earlier you involve people in the change, the more likely you'll mitigate any resistance they might feel. When people help to frame the problem that a change program is seeking to solve *and* have input on how the change will be implemented, they're more likely to understand their own role in the change process and to feel a sense of ownership in the process. And that goes a long way toward reducing resistance.

- **Proactively identify those who have something to lose as a result of the change and anticipate how they might respond.** Start thinking of ways to ease their concerns, for example, by providing training or involving them in designing new processes.

- **Help them find new roles in your group or somewhere else in the organization.** Look for roles that represent genuine contributions and that mitigate their losses.

Also, as you consider resisters, be sure to evaluate what part *you* may be playing in causing their resistance. It's possible that your approach to managing change or your leadership style may be threatening to others, thereby causing unnecessary friction and

Steps for Addressing Resistance to Change

1. **Encourage people to openly express their thoughts and feelings about the change.** Create an environment that fosters open communication and exchange of ideas. Actively reach out to employees—using informal hallway conversations, more formal one-on-one meetings, e-mail, and other channels—and ask them how they're managing the change effort.

2. **When resistance occurs, listen carefully.** While it's important to explain the benefits of a change program, employees who are resistant to the change don't always want to hear an explanation of why the change is necessary. Instead, work to understand their resistance by exploring their concerns and by taking their feelings and comments seriously.

3. **Treat resistance as a problem to solve, not as a character flaw.** Resisters may provide valuable information about a change program—information that you may not be aware of. For example, a resister may reveal an unanticipated consequence of a projected change that could result in a potential threat to either the unit or the organization. Instead of dismissing the resister as someone who is negative or inflexible, try to understand his or her rationale and sources of motivation. Doing so can open up new, unexpected possibilities for realizing change.

4. **Once you understand the nature of their concerns, bring people together to discuss and deal with the perceived problems.** If people feel that they've been heard and have had opportunities to discuss problems and suggest solutions, they are more

likely to support the decisions surrounding the change initiative. Address all concerns head-on and provide people with as much information as possible.

---

conflict. "Steps for Addressing Resistance to Change" gives additional suggestions for dealing with this particular challenge.

If you want to make enemies, try to change something.
—Woodrow Wilson

What You COULD Do

Remember Penelope's questions about how to deal with Charlie's resistance to the change program?

Here's what the mentor suggests:

Penelope should ask to meet with Charlie to talk more directly about his concerns. While this may seem like she's putting him on the spot, asking to meet with him so she can talk openly about his reactions to the change program is the best course of action. It is important for Penelope to listen to Charlie's concerns and examine the motives and rationale behind his resistance. The information that she receives may provide valuable insights into the change effort that she is leading. For example, Charlie might point out a serious flaw in the way the training in the new system is being presented—a flaw that Penelope wasn't aware of. This, in turn, might uncover new opportunities to improve the change effort.

Maintaining Your Effectiveness During Change

So far, we've talked about how to lead change successfully by, in part, managing change's disruptive impact on your employees. But just like your employees, you also will be affected by the very change initiatives you're leading. Change is difficult for everyone—those managing it, and those affected by it. If you let a change initiative wear you down, you won't be able to lead it successfully. Here are some ideas for managing change's impact on you.

Secure your physical and emotional well-being

Because change programs are almost always disruptive, they can take both a physical and an emotional toll on those involved. While it's important to help your employees adapt and adjust to change, it's equally important for you to take stock of your own reactions to the change program and reduce any feelings of stress and anxiety that you may experience during the transition.

Since adapting to change can be arduous, you need to maintain your physical well-being and nurture your psyche. For example:

- Get enough sleep.

- Pay attention to diet and exercise.

- Take occasional breaks at the office.

- Relax with friends.

- Engage in hobbies.

These are not forms of escapism. Rather, they are practical ways of exerting control over your life during a period of flux.

Take action to overcome a sense of powerlessness

If a change program has been introduced without your input or prior knowledge, you may experience feelings of powerlessness. One antidote to this sensation is to work with your boss to define your role in the new direction the company is taking. Doing so ensures that your expectations are aligned with those of your supervisor's and that you have some control over the changes taking place.

Another antidote to feeling powerless is to establish a sense of personal control in other areas of your life. For example, if you've always wanted to learn Spanish, you might enroll in a Spanish immersion class. You'll gain a sense of purpose as well as grow in areas outside your organizational life.

Another antidote is to avoid taking on other efforts that sap your energy. You may find that the best way to regain control is to just relax, think, and ponder the events that have transpired.

"Steps for Assessing Your Reactions to Change" shows actions you can take to gauge how you might respond to a change initiative. By taking stock of your reactions, you can better prepare yourself to manage them.

Balance your emotional investments

Another way people bring greater stability to their lives during times of change is to balance the emotional investment they put into their work (how they perform their jobs and manage their relationships with others) with the emotional investment they put

Steps for Assessing Your Reactions to Change

1. **Reflect on past changes that you've experienced.** Consider positive and negative changes that you've undergone either on the job or in your personal life. Recall how you felt during each of those changes. Were you excited? Shocked? Angry? Feeling a mix of different emotions?

2. **Analyze your reactions to those changes.** For those times when you reacted positively to change, identify the factors surrounding the change that led to those positive reactions. Did you support the change because you thought it was the right course of action? Because you respected the people mandating or leading the change? Because you thought the change initiative might result in some form of personal gain?

   For those times that you reacted negatively, identify the causes of your frustration, shock, or other negative reactions. Did you resist the change because you thought it was unnecessary or would make the situation worse? Because you weren't involved in the planning and/or implementation of the change initiatives? Because you didn't want to let go of the status quo?

3. **Evaluate what you did to successfully manage your reactions to those changes.** What worked well and why? What didn't work well and why? What steps could you take to improve the way you react to change? Answers to these questions will prepare you better for the next time you encounter change.

into their personal lives (family and social relationships as well as civic and religious interests).

Often, when change programs are launched, managers pour all of their emotional energy into addressing workplace concerns. But it can take weeks or even months for these issues or problems to be resolved, during which little time is left to nurture personal relationships and interests.

To avoid throwing your life off balance, strive to invest roughly equal amounts of emotion in the workplace and in your personal life, even though doing so may seem difficult. When a change program disrupts one or more activities you usually perform in the workplace, you can draw emotional support from and find stability in your personal life.

Anticipate additional change

Maintaining a sense of balance and stability while going through a change program is difficult for anyone. Perhaps the best mechanism for coping with change is anticipating it. If you recognize that change takes time, that it has a powerful emotional impact, and that you have the strength to manage the transition, you'll position yourself to navigate the challenges that typically accompany a change effort. And the more skillfully you navigate those challenges, the more effective you'll be as a leader of change in your organization.

Change is the law of life. And those who look only to the past or present are certain to miss the future.
    —John F. Kennedy

Tips and Tools

Tools for Managing Change

Self-Assessment for Managers of Change

The questions below relate to characteristics and skills of successful managers of change. Use the questions to evaluate whether you possess these attributes. Use the results to see where you might focus to strengthen your management skills.

Question	Yes	No
1. Are you accepted by others as trustworthy?		
2. Do others perceive you as competent?		
3. Do you understand the long-range strategy for your unit and organization?		
4. Can you articulate the concerns of your organization's most powerful groups?		
5. Do you know how to develop a clear and compelling vision?		
6. Are you able to articulate the vision of your unit or organization (whether created by your or others)?		
7. Do you know who your key stakeholders are when implementing a change program?		
8. Do you get buy-in from your stakeholders before you move forward on change initiatives?		
9. Do you communicate the scope and benefits of a change program to your key stakeholders and team in terms of what is important to them?		
10. Do you involve those who will be most affected by the change in the planning and implementation processes?		
11. Do you push decision making down to the lowest possible levels in your unit or organization?		
12. Do you know how to motivate others to achieve a change program's goals?		
13. Do you know where to turn for the resources you need?		
14. Are you willing to take calculated risks?		
15. Are you comfortable with a certain level of disruption and conflict?		

16. Do you actively listen to others' concerns?		
17. Do you see and diagnose problems from the perspective of the people to be affected by the change?		
18. When pursuing a goal, do you maintain a positive, focused attitude, despite obstacles?		
19. Do you eliminate barriers that stand in the way of a change program?		
20. Are you aware of/can you describe how your own patterns of behavior have an impact on others?		

If you answered "**yes**" to most of these questions, you possess many of the characteristics and skills needed to be a successful manager of change.

If you answered "**no**" to some or many of these questions, you may want to consider how you can further develop these management skills and attributes.

Worksheet for Communicating Change

Use this tool to collect and disseminate information about a change program.

Part I: Gather Information About the Change Initiative

What is the change program and what are its goals?

Why is the change program taking place?

What is the scope of the change program?

What hurdles stand in the way of implementing the change program?

What are the criteria for success, and how will success be measured?

How will people be rewarded for success?

Part II: Identify Key Stakeholders and How/What You Will Communicate to Them		
Stakeholder	**Communication approach**	**Information that you will communicate (in addition to information in Part I)**
Name: Title: Responsibilities:	___ One-on-one meetings ___ Group meetings ___ One-on-one phone calls ___ Conference phone calls ___ E-mails ___ Memos ___ Other:	Benefits of change program to this stakeholder: Disadvantages of change program to this stakeholder:
Name: Title: Responsibilities:	___ One-on-one meetings ___ Group meetings ___ One-on-one phone calls ___ Conference phone calls ___ E-mails ___ Memos ___ Other:	Benefits of change program to this stakeholder: Disadvantages of change program to this stakeholder:
Name: Title: Responsibilities:	___ One-on-one meetings ___ Group meetings ___ One-on-one phone calls ___ Conference phone calls ___ E-mails ___ Memos ___ Other:	Benefits of change program to this stakeholder: Disadvantages of change program to this stakeholder:
Name: Title: Responsibilities:	___ One-on-one meetings ___ Group meetings ___ One-on-one phone calls ___ Conference phone calls ___ E-mails ___ Memos ___ Other:	Benefits of change program to this stakeholder: Disadvantages of change program to this stakeholder:

Worksheet for Addressing Resistance to Change

Use this tool to record the reasons why people are resistant to change and determine the next steps for addressing this resistance.

What comments have you heard or what behaviors have you seen that indicate people are resistant to the change program?	What do you think the underlying motivations for these reactions are?
Examples: • *"I don't think our group should be merged with another group."* • *Everyone is quiet in staff meetings.*	*Examples:* • *People prefer the status quo or feel that change will mean personal loss—in terms of security, money, status, or friends.* • *People are not willing to raise issues with me.*

Steps for Addressing Resistance		
Yes	No	
☐	☐	Have you talked one-on-one with individuals who are resistant to change to better understand their reactions?
☐	☐	Did you encourage them to express their thoughts and feelings openly?
☐	☐	Did you explore their concerns by asking clarifying questions?
☐	☐	Did you listen carefully to their responses and take their comments seriously?
☐	☐	Have you communicated the benefits of the change in terms of what might be of value to them?
☐	☐	Have you incorporated their suggestions into the plan to improve it?
☐	☐	Have you explored ways to engage these individuals in the planning and implementation processes so that they feel more invested in the change program?
☐	☐	Did you consider the ways in which *you* may be adding to their feelings of resistance?
		If you answer "no" to any of the questions above, you may want to rethink how you're addressing resistance to the change program.

Worksheet for Overcoming Obstacles to Change

Use this tool to keep your team focused on the most important problems standing in the way of implementing change. For each obstacle to your team's progress, list and evaluate options for overcoming it. Also list any allies, additional resources, or special training your team members will need in order to collaborate most effectively on the chosen option.

Obstacle to team's progress	Options for overcoming the obstacle	Rank the options (1 = most promising; 5 = least promising)	Allies, resources, special training

Test Yourself

This section offers ten multiple-choice questions to help you identify your baseline knowledge of the essentials of managing change. Answers to the questions are given at the end of the test.

1. Who should initiate organizational change?

   a. The CEO.

   b. Senior executives one level below the CEO.

   c. Managers at all levels in the organization.

2. A merger or acquisition represents what type of change program?

   a. Structural.

   b. Cost-cutting.

   c. Cultural.

3. If your team isn't primed for transition, how might you help it become change-ready?

   a. Create short-term wins.

   b. Develop a strong change-implementation plan.

   c. Encourage collaborative work in your team.

4. What's the first step in leading a change initiative?

    a. Create a vision of the better future that the change effort will deliver.

    b. Define the business problem that the change is supposed to address.

    c. Identify who'll lead the change effort.

5. True or false? During a change initiative, managers should focus their attention on generating near-term wins.

    a. True.

    b. False.

6. Which of the following is a defining characteristic of an effective implementation plan?

    a. It has very ambitious goals so people are challenged to improve performance.

    b. It's flexible and open to revision.

    c. It's created by a small group of highly experienced managers.

7. What's the best way to communicate about a change program to employees?

    a. Once a week during staff meetings, to emphasize face-to-face interaction.

    b. Every other week by e-mail, to increase speed and reach of communication.

c. As often as necessary and through as many channels as possible to get the message across.

8. True or false? It's important to explain how people will be rewarded for carrying out a change initiative.

a. True.

b. False.

9. An employee has expressed resistance to a change program you've proposed. What should be your first response?

a. Encourage him to express his thoughts and then listen to his responses.

b. Move him to a different group so he doesn't sabotage the program.

c. Let him work through his feelings on his own, as people need time to adjust.

10. Which of the following are examples of enabling structures?

a. Implementation plans.

b. Training programs.

c. Change visions.

Answers to test questions

1, c. Managers from all levels of a company can and should initiate change. Change is about looking for opportunities to improve business performance. Anyone—regardless of professional title or position in the organizational hierarchy—can identify such opportunities.

2, a. A merger or acquisition is an example of a structural change program. Such programs attempt to reconfigure the organization in order to achieve greater overall performance.

3, c. By developing more collaborative approaches to how everyday business is handled—for example, pushing decision making down to the lowest levels possible, sharing information freely, and encouraging two-way communication—you can prime your team for transition.

4, b. The starting point of any effective change effort is a clear definition of the business problem you want to address through the change. Problem identification answers the most important question employees will ask: why must we undergo change? Your answer lays the foundation for motivating your employees to embrace change. Thus, it must be convincing.

5, a. During a change initiative, managers should focus on near-term, results-driven programs. For example, a company might create the following goal: "Within the next twelve months, we will increase revenues by 5 percent." Such programs show people that small gains in a larger change effort are achievable and that their hard work can have a direct impact on overall business performance.

6, b. Change programs seldom follow their planned trajectories or timetables. Thus, a good implementation plan is flexible and open to revision as needed. It's also concise and coherent; created by people at all affected levels; structured in manageable, achievable sections; and clear in its definitions of roles and responsibilities.

7, c. There is no such thing as overcommunicating information about a change program. Share information as often as necessary and in as many ways possible, for example, through e-mail, one-on-one meetings, or a monthly newsletter. That way, employees will hear about the purpose and goals of the change program over and over again, increasing the likelihood that they will embrace the change initiative.

8, a. People need incentives for taking on the added work and disruptions that change requires. Be very clear about what the criteria for success are, how success will be measured, and how individuals will be rewarded for progress toward change goals.

9, a. Exploring the person's concerns and taking his comments seriously show that you want to better understand the nature of his resistance and work with him as an active partner in the change program. Resisters are commonly viewed as inflexible, unaccommodating, and lacking team spirit. While some resisters can undermine a change effort, they don't all possess such negative attributes. Find ways to get to the root of the resistance. Then try to redirect the individual's energy in support of the change effort.

10, b. A training program is an enabling structure because it provides employees with opportunities to improve their skills so they can contribute more effectively to the change initiative. Pilot programs and reward systems are other examples of enabling structures. Pilot programs give people an opportunity to experiment with projects before they are rolled out more broadly. Reward systems acknowledge people for achieving results and demonstrating behaviors that support the change program.

To Learn More

Articles

Bunker, Kerry A., and Michael Wakefield. "Leading in Times of Change." *Harvard Management Update*, May 2006.

> During change, leaders must perform a delicate balancing act: they have to make tough decisions without losing sight of the emotions and concerns of employees. To do this, the authors argue, requires managing the tension between seemingly opposing tasks and capabilities; for instance: "Show a sense of urgency" and "Demonstrate realistic patience." The article guides you in striking the right balance to drive successful change. Includes the graphic "The Transition Leadership Wheel."

Garvin, David A., and Michael A. Roberto. "Change Through Persuasion." *Harvard Business Review* OnPoint Enhanced Edition. Boston: Harvard Business School Publishing, January 2006.

> In this article, the authors contend that to make change stick, leaders must conduct an effective persuasion campaign—one that begins weeks or months before the turnaround plan is set in concrete. Turnaround leaders must convince people that the organization is truly on its deathbed or, at the very least, that radical changes are required if the organization is to survive and thrive. And they must demonstrate through word and

deed that they are the right leaders with the right plan. Accomplishing all this calls for a four-part communications strategy. Using the example of the dramatic turnaround at Boston's Beth Israel Deaconess Medical Center, the authors elucidate the inner workings of a successful change effort.

Herrin, Angelia. "You're Ready for Top-Line Growth—Are Your Employees?" *Harvard Management Update*, April 2004.

A change in strategy is not enough. Employees need to prioritize their work and approach resources in new ways. Managers can smooth and speed changes by understanding that a successful transition requires the completion of three phases: the ending, the neutral zone, and the new beginning. Change management expert William Bridges explains how managers can accomplish this.

Hirschhorn, Larry. "Campaigning for Change." *Harvard Business Review* OnPoint Enhanced Edition. Boston: Harvard Business School Publishing, 2002.

Successful change programs have one thing in common: they employ three distinct but linked campaigns—political, marketing, and military. A political campaign creates a coalition strong enough to support and guide the initiative. A marketing campaign must go beyond simply publicizing the initiative's benefits: it focuses on listening to ideas that bubble up from the field as well as on working with lead customers to design the initiative. A clearly articulated theme for the transformation program must also be developed. A military campaign deploys executives' scarce resources of attention and time. Successful managers launch all three campaigns simultaneously. The three always feed on one another, and if any one campaign is not properly implemented, the change initiative is bound to fail.

Kotter, John P. "Leading Change: Why Transformation Efforts Fail." *Harvard Business Review* OnPoint Enhanced Edition. Boston: Harvard Business School Publishing, 2000.

During the past decade, the author has watched more than a hundred companies try to remake themselves into better competitors. Their efforts have gone under many banners: total quality management, reengineering, right-sizing, restructuring, cultural change, and turnarounds. A few of these efforts have been very successful. A few have been utter failures. Most fall somewhere in between, with a distinct tilt toward the lower end of the scale. Among the lessons learned: change involves numerous phases that, together, usually take a long time; and skipping steps only creates an illusion of speed and never produces a satisfying result.

Books

Abrahamson, Eric. *Change Without Pain: How Managers Can Overcome Initiative Overload, Organizational Chaos, and Employee Burnout.* Boston: Harvard Business School Press, 2003.

Columbia Business School Professor Abrahamson argues that although change is necessary for companies to grow and prosper, many organizations have blindly taken the mandate too far. The "creative destruction" advocated by change champions has resulted in a painful cycle of initiative overload, change-related chaos, and widespread employee cynicism. To reverse this cycle, Abrahamson says, companies must learn to change how they change. Drawing on a decade of research and dozens of company examples, this book offers a positive new approach to change called "creative recombination." Rather than obliterating and then reinventing, creative recombination seeks a sustainable, repeatable transformation by reconfiguring the people, structures, culture, processes, and networks the company already has.

Kotter, John P., and Dan S. Cohen. *The Heart of Change: Real-Life Stories of How People Change Their Organizations*. Boston: Harvard Business School Press, 2002.

For individuals in every walk of life and in every stage of change, this compact, no-nonsense book captures both the heart—and the "how"—of successful change. Organizations are forced to change faster and more radically. How are companies faring in meeting these challenges, and what can we learn from their experiences? Although most organizations believe change happens by making people think differently, Kotter and Cohen say the key lies more in making them feel differently. They introduce a new dynamic—"see-feel-change"—that sparks and fuels action by showing people potent reasons for change that charge their emotions.

eLearning Programs

Harvard Business School Publishing. *Case in Point*. Boston: Harvard Business School Publishing, 2004.

Case in Point is a flexible set of online cases, designed to help prepare middle- and senior-level managers for a variety of leadership challenges. These short, reality-based scenarios provide sophisticated content to create a focused view into the realities of the life of a leader. Your managers will experience: Aligning Strategy, Removing Implementation Barriers, Overseeing Change, Anticipating Risk, Ethical Decisions, Building a Business Case, Cultivating Customer Loyalty, Emotional Intelligence, Developing a Global Perspective, Fostering Innovation, Defining Problems, Selecting Solutions, Managing Difficult Interactions, The Coach's Role, Delegating for Growth, Managing Creativity, Influencing Others, Managing Performance, Providing Feedback, and Retaining Talent.

Harvard Business School Publishing. *Managing Change.* Boston: Harvard Business School Publishing, 2000.

Based on the research and writings of today's top leadership and change experts, this program explores how managers can balance, pace, and roll out change initiatives. It will help you analyze the organizational dynamics of change, choose the right strategies, and lead change initiatives for bottom-line results.

Harvard Business School Publishing. *What Is a Leader?* Boston: Harvard Business School Publishing, 2001.

Based on the research and writings of today's top leadership experts, this program explores what it takes to be a successful leader. You will analyze where you are and what you need to do to move from a competent manager to an exceptional leader.

Sources for Managing Change

The following sources aided in development of this book:

Davis, Brian L. et al. *Successful Manager's Handbook*. Minneapolis, MN: Personnel Decisions International, 1992.

Deal, Terrence E., and M. K. Key. *Corporate Celebration: Play, Purpose, and Profit at Work*. San Francisco: Berrett-Koehler, 1998.

Hakim, Cliff. *We Are All Self-Employed: The New Social Contract for Working in a Changed World*. San Francisco: Berrett-Koehler, 1994.

Harvard Business School Publishing. *Managing Change and Transition*. Boston: Harvard Business School Press, 2003.

Hill, Linda A. "Power Dynamics in Organizations." Harvard Business School Case Note 9-494-083, 1994.

Jeffreys, J. Shep. *Coping with Workplace Change: Dealing with Loss and Grief*. Menlo Park, CA: Crisp Publications, Inc., 1995.

Jick, Todd D. "Note on the Recipients of Change." Harvard Business School Case Note 9-491-039, 1996.

Jick, Todd D. "The Challenge of Change." Harvard Business School Case Note 9-490-016, 1989.

Kotter, John P. *Leading Change*. Boston: Harvard Business School Press, 1996.

Kotter, John P., and Walter Kiechel. "How to Get Aboard a Major Change Effort: An Interview with John Kotter." *Harvard Management Update*, September 1996.

Vogt, Judith F., and Kenneth L. Murrell. *Empowerment in Organizations: How to Spark Exceptional Performance*. San Diego, CA: Pfeiffer, 1990.

Notes

Notes

Notes

Notes

Notes

Notes

Notes

Notes

Notes

Notes

Notes

Notes

Notes

Notes

Notes

How to Order

Harvard Business School Press publications are available world-wide from your local bookseller or online retailer.

You can also call:
1-800-668-6780

Our product consultants are available to help you 8:00 a.m.–6:00 p.m., Monday–Friday, Eastern Time. Outside the U.S. and Canada, call: 617-783-7450.

Please call about special discounts for quantities greater than ten.

You can order online at:
www.HBSPress.org